PRINCEWILL LAGANG

Unleashing the Cloud: Larry Ellison's Impact on Enterprise Computing and Database Revolution

First published by PRINCEWILL LAGANG 2023

Copyright © 2023 by Princewill Lagang

All rights reserved. No part of this publication may be reproduced, stored or transmitted in any form or by any means, electronic, mechanical, photocopying, recording, scanning, or otherwise without written permission from the publisher. It is illegal to copy this book, post it to a website, or distribute it by any other means without permission.

Princewill Lagang asserts the moral right to be identified as the author of this work.

First edition

This book was professionally typeset on Reedsy.
Find out more at reedsy.com

Contents

1. Unleashing the Cloud: Larry Ellison's Impact on Enterprise...   1
2. Oracle's Database Dominance: Powering the Backbone of...   4
3. Cloud Revolution: Oracle's Odyssey in Transforming...   7
4. Revolutionizing Business Applications: Oracle's Impact on...   10
5. Oracle's Ecosystem: Partnerships, Acquisitions, and...   13
6. Oracle's Vision for the Future: Emerging Technologies and...   16
7. Oracle's Global Impact: Social Responsibility, Diversity,...   19
8. Navigating Challenges and Future Horizons: Oracle in a...   22
9. Reflections and Conclusions: Oracle's Enduring Legacy and...   25
10. Beyond the Horizon: Exploring Emerging Trends and Future...   28
11. The Human Element: Oracle's Impact on Workforce Dynamics and...   31
12. The Global Impact of Oracle: A Retrospective and Prospective...   34
13. Summary   37

1

Unleashing the Cloud: Larry Ellison's Impact on Enterprise Computing and Database Revolution

Introduction:

In the realm of enterprise computing, few figures have left as indelible a mark as Larry Ellison, the visionary co-founder of Oracle Corporation. This chapter embarks on a journey through the transformative landscape of enterprise computing, exploring Ellison's pivotal role in reshaping the industry and spearheading the evolution of databases into the era of the cloud.

1.1 The Genesis of a Visionary:

To understand Larry Ellison's impact, we must first delve into the genesis of his visionary mindset. Born in 1944, Ellison's early life was marked by an insatiable curiosity and an innate passion for technology. Raised in Chicago and later migrating to California, Ellison's experiences laid the foundation for a maverick who would challenge the status quo of enterprise computing.

1.2 The Birth of Oracle Corporation:

The narrative pivots to the early 1970s when Larry Ellison, along with Bob Miner and Ed Oates, co-founded Oracle Corporation. Focused initially on relational databases, Oracle's mission was to create a robust and efficient database management system (DBMS). This section explores the challenges they faced, the innovative solutions they implemented, and the gradual emergence of Oracle as a trailblazer in the database domain.

1.3 Relational Databases: A Paradigm Shift:

The chapter then delves into the significance of relational databases, elucidating how Oracle's technology revolutionized data management. By introducing the concept of organizing data into tables and enabling powerful query capabilities, Oracle's relational database management system (RDBMS) became a linchpin for businesses seeking to streamline their operations.

1.4 Larry Ellison's Strategic Vision:

At the core of Oracle's success was Larry Ellison's strategic vision. This section examines Ellison's foresight in anticipating the needs of enterprises for scalable, reliable, and secure databases. His emphasis on innovation and adaptability positioned Oracle as an industry leader, setting the stage for the next frontier: the cloud.

1.5 The Cloud Computing Revolution:

As the narrative unfolds, the chapter navigates through the evolution of cloud computing and its profound impact on enterprise IT. Larry Ellison's forward-looking stance on the cloud as the future of computing marked a paradigm shift, and Oracle's transition to cloud services positioned the company at the forefront of this technological revolution.

1.6 Oracle's Cloud Offerings:

The chapter culminates in an exploration of Oracle's cloud offerings. From infrastructure as a service (IaaS) to platform as a service (PaaS) and software as a service (SaaS), Oracle's comprehensive suite of cloud solutions reflects Ellison's commitment to providing end-to-end services that empower businesses to thrive in the digital age.

Conclusion:

The inaugural chapter encapsulates the journey of Larry Ellison from a tech enthusiast to a pioneering force in enterprise computing. It sets the stage for a deeper exploration of Ellison's impact on the technological landscape, paving the way for subsequent chapters that delve into specific aspects of Oracle's influence on databases, cloud computing, and the future of enterprise IT.

2

Oracle's Database Dominance: Powering the Backbone of Enterprise Operations

Introduction:

Building on the foundation laid in Chapter 1, this chapter delves deeper into the realm of databases, focusing on Oracle's ascent to dominance and its pivotal role in shaping the backbone of enterprise operations. From the inception of Oracle's database technology to its continuous evolution, this chapter unveils the intricacies of how Oracle's database solutions became synonymous with reliability, scalability, and innovation.

2.1 The Evolution of Oracle Database Technology:

The chapter commences with a historical overview of Oracle's database technology. Tracing the evolution from the early releases to the sophisticated Oracle Database of today, the narrative highlights key milestones, technological breakthroughs, and the relentless commitment to enhancing database capabilities.

2.2 Oracle's Relational Database Management System (RDBMS):

At the heart of Oracle's success lies its robust Relational Database Management System (RDBMS). This section explores the architecture and functionalities that distinguish Oracle's RDBMS, emphasizing its role in enabling organizations to efficiently store, retrieve, and manage vast amounts of structured data.

2.3 Oracle's Impact on Data Warehousing:

The chapter extends its focus to Oracle's influence on data warehousing, elucidating how the company pioneered solutions for efficiently storing and analyzing massive volumes of data. Oracle's data warehousing technologies, including Oracle Exadata, revolutionized the way organizations harness insights from their data, fostering a data-driven decision-making culture.

2.4 Scalability and Performance:

Oracle's commitment to scalability and performance has been a cornerstone of its database solutions. This section examines how Oracle's technologies have consistently pushed the boundaries, allowing enterprises to handle ever-increasing data workloads while maintaining optimal performance.

2.5 Security and Reliability:

Security is paramount in the world of databases, and Oracle has been at the forefront of developing robust security features. This part of the chapter delves into Oracle's commitment to data integrity, confidentiality, and availability, showcasing how their databases became a trusted fortress for sensitive enterprise information.

2.6 Oracle in Mission-Critical Environments:

Oracle's database technology has been instrumental in supporting mission-critical applications across industries. This section explores real-world examples of Oracle databases powering financial transactions, healthcare systems, and other essential functions, underscoring the reliability and resilience of Oracle's solutions.

2.7 Oracle's Role in Digital Transformation:

The chapter concludes by examining Oracle's pivotal role in facilitating digital transformation for enterprises. By providing a scalable and flexible database foundation, Oracle has empowered organizations to adapt to rapidly evolving business landscapes and capitalize on emerging technologies.

Conclusion:

Chapter 2 provides a comprehensive exploration of Oracle's database dominance and its profound impact on enterprise operations. From the foundational principles of Oracle's RDBMS to its role in mission-critical environments, the chapter sets the stage for subsequent sections that will further unravel Oracle's influence on cloud computing and the broader landscape of enterprise technology.

3

Cloud Revolution: Oracle's Odyssey in Transforming Enterprise IT

Introduction:

Building upon the narrative of Oracle's database prowess, Chapter 3 delves into the transformative journey of Oracle Corporation in navigating the cloud revolution. Larry Ellison's visionary stance on the cloud as the future of computing laid the groundwork for Oracle's strategic pivot. This chapter explores Oracle's foray into cloud services, its impact on enterprise IT, and the innovations that have reshaped the technological landscape.

3.1 Larry Ellison's Vision for the Cloud:

The chapter begins by revisiting Larry Ellison's early articulation of the cloud's potential and his conviction that cloud computing would redefine the way businesses operate. Ellison's foresight into the agility, scalability, and cost-effectiveness of cloud services became the catalyst for Oracle's strategic shift.

3.2 Oracle Cloud Offerings:

A detailed exploration of Oracle's cloud offerings takes center stage. From Infrastructure as a Service (IaaS) to Platform as a Service (PaaS) and Software as a Service (SaaS), this section outlines Oracle's comprehensive suite of cloud solutions. It delves into the features, benefits, and industry applications, showcasing how Oracle's cloud ecosystem caters to diverse enterprise needs.

3.3 Oracle Cloud Infrastructure (OCI):

Within the broader spectrum of cloud offerings, Oracle Cloud Infrastructure (OCI) emerges as a critical component. This part of the chapter unpacks the architecture, scalability, and performance capabilities of OCI, illustrating how Oracle has endeavored to provide a robust and reliable foundation for businesses migrating to the cloud.

3.4 Cloud Security and Compliance:

Security in the cloud is a paramount concern for enterprises. The chapter examines Oracle's commitment to cloud security, including advanced encryption, identity management, and compliance features. It highlights how Oracle's cloud solutions are designed to address the evolving challenges of data protection and regulatory compliance.

3.5 Oracle Autonomous Database:

A focal point of Oracle's cloud strategy is the Autonomous Database. This section explores the groundbreaking features of the Autonomous Database, emphasizing its self-driving, self-securing, and self-repairing capabilities. The narrative underscores how Oracle's autonomous technology represents a paradigm shift in database management.

3.6 Cloud Integration and Innovation:

Oracle's cloud journey extends beyond infrastructure and databases; it encompasses a commitment to fostering innovation. This part of the chapter explores Oracle's initiatives in cloud integration, artificial intelligence, machine learning, and emerging technologies, showcasing how Oracle empowers businesses to stay at the forefront of digital transformation.

3.7 Case Studies: Oracle Cloud Success Stories:

The chapter concludes by spotlighting real-world case studies of organizations that have embraced Oracle Cloud and realized tangible benefits. These success stories illustrate the diverse ways in which Oracle's cloud solutions have catalyzed business growth, efficiency gains, and competitive advantage.

Conclusion:

Chapter 3 provides a comprehensive overview of Oracle's odyssey in transforming enterprise IT through cloud computing. From Larry Ellison's visionary insights to Oracle's diverse cloud offerings and success stories, this chapter sets the stage for a deeper exploration of Oracle's ongoing impact on the ever-evolving landscape of enterprise technology.

4

Revolutionizing Business Applications: Oracle's Impact on Enterprise Software

Introduction:

As Oracle Corporation continues its journey through the dynamic landscape of enterprise technology, Chapter 4 focuses on the company's profound impact on business applications. From Enterprise Resource Planning (ERP) to Customer Relationship Management (CRM), Oracle's suite of software solutions has played a pivotal role in reshaping how organizations operate and engage with their customers.

4.1 Oracle's Enterprise Resource Planning (ERP) Solutions:

The chapter begins by delving into Oracle's contributions to Enterprise Resource Planning (ERP). It explores how Oracle's ERP solutions have streamlined and integrated core business processes, from finance and human resources to supply chain management. The narrative highlights Oracle's commitment to providing end-to-end solutions that enhance operational efficiency and decision-making.

4.2 Oracle's Customer Relationship Management (CRM) Innovations:

The spotlight then shifts to Oracle's innovations in Customer Relationship Management (CRM). This section unravels the evolution of Oracle's CRM solutions, emphasizing their role in helping businesses build and maintain strong customer relationships. From sales automation to marketing and customer service, Oracle's CRM offerings have become integral to fostering customer-centric enterprises.

4.3 Cloud-Based Applications: SaaS and PaaS:

A significant aspect of Oracle's impact on enterprise software is its transition to cloud-based applications. The chapter explores Oracle's Software as a Service (SaaS) and Platform as a Service (PaaS) offerings, illustrating how businesses can leverage these cloud-based solutions to enhance flexibility, scalability, and accessibility while reducing infrastructure complexities.

4.4 Oracle Fusion Applications:

At the heart of Oracle's cloud-based applications lies Oracle Fusion Applications. This section provides an in-depth exploration of Fusion Applications, showcasing their modular and integrated nature. The narrative underscores how Oracle Fusion Applications bridge the gap between traditional on-premises solutions and the agility of cloud-based platforms.

4.5 Industry-Specific Solutions:

Oracle's impact on enterprise software extends beyond generic applications; the company has developed industry-specific solutions tailored to unique business needs. This part of the chapter highlights Oracle's vertical expertise, demonstrating how industries such as healthcare, finance, and manufacturing benefit from specialized Oracle software.

4.6 Integration of Emerging Technologies:

Oracle has been at the forefront of integrating emerging technologies into its business applications. This section explores how Oracle incorporates artificial intelligence, machine learning, and Internet of Things (IoT) capabilities into its software suite, enabling businesses to harness the power of data-driven insights and automation.

4.7 Case Studies: Transformative Impact on Businesses:

The chapter concludes by presenting case studies that showcase how organizations across diverse industries have experienced transformative changes through Oracle's business applications. These real-world examples underscore the tangible benefits of Oracle's software solutions in enhancing operational efficiency, driving innovation, and fostering business growth.

Conclusion:

Chapter 4 sheds light on Oracle's revolutionary impact on enterprise software, emphasizing its role in shaping ERP, CRM, and industry-specific solutions. From on-premises applications to cloud-based innovations, Oracle continues to be a trailblazer, empowering businesses to navigate the complexities of the modern digital landscape. The chapter sets the stage for further exploration into Oracle's ongoing contributions to the evolving landscape of enterprise technology.

5

Oracle's Ecosystem: Partnerships, Acquisitions, and Community

Introduction:

As Oracle Corporation has evolved, so has its ecosystem. Chapter 5 delves into the intricate web of partnerships, strategic acquisitions, and the vibrant community that surrounds Oracle. This ecosystem plays a crucial role in shaping the company's trajectory, influencing its innovation, and contributing to the broader landscape of enterprise technology.

5.1 Strategic Partnerships:

The chapter begins by examining Oracle's strategic partnerships with other technology giants, industry leaders, and innovative startups. It explores how these collaborations have facilitated the integration of complementary technologies, expanded Oracle's reach into new markets, and fostered a culture of co-innovation within the industry.

5.2 Oracle's Acquisitions Strategy:

A significant aspect of Oracle's growth lies in its strategic acquisitions. This section provides an in-depth analysis of key acquisitions that have bolstered Oracle's portfolio, expanded its technological capabilities, and positioned the company at the forefront of emerging trends. From database technologies to cloud services and applications, Oracle's acquisitions have been instrumental in shaping its diverse offerings.

5.3 Oracle's Impact on Open Source:

The narrative then shifts to Oracle's involvement in the open-source community. This section explores Oracle's contributions to open-source projects, its support for developer communities, and the balance it strikes between proprietary solutions and open-source initiatives. It also examines Oracle's role in popular open-source databases and tools.

5.4 Oracle User Groups and Community Engagement:

An integral part of Oracle's ecosystem is its vibrant community of users, developers, and enthusiasts. The chapter highlights the various user groups, forums, and events that foster collaboration, knowledge sharing, and feedback loops. Oracle's commitment to community engagement is explored, illustrating how it influences product development and supports users in maximizing the value of Oracle technologies.

5.5 Cloud Partner Ecosystem:

With the rise of cloud computing, Oracle has cultivated a robust ecosystem of cloud partners. This section outlines how Oracle collaborates with technology partners, system integrators, and independent software vendors to deliver comprehensive solutions to customers. The narrative emphasizes the mutual benefits derived from this ecosystem, driving innovation and expanding market reach.

5.6 Oracle's Commitment to Sustainability:

As environmental consciousness becomes increasingly vital, the chapter explores Oracle's commitment to sustainability. From data center efficiency initiatives to incorporating environmentally friendly practices in its operations, Oracle's approach to sustainability is examined. The narrative underscores how Oracle contributes to addressing environmental challenges within the technology sector.

5.7 The Future of Oracle's Ecosystem:

The chapter concludes by offering insights into the future trajectory of Oracle's ecosystem. It speculates on potential trends in partnerships, acquisitions, community engagement, and sustainability efforts. By examining Oracle's current strategies and industry trends, the chapter sets the stage for anticipating the company's role in shaping the future of enterprise technology.

Conclusion:

Chapter 5 provides a comprehensive exploration of Oracle's ecosystem, encompassing strategic partnerships, acquisitions, community engagement, and sustainability initiatives. As Oracle continues to evolve, its dynamic ecosystem remains a key driver of innovation and collaboration in the ever-changing landscape of enterprise technology. The chapter lays the foundation for further understanding Oracle's holistic impact on the industry.

6

Oracle's Vision for the Future: Emerging Technologies and Industry Trends

Introduction:

As Oracle Corporation stands at the forefront of enterprise technology, Chapter 6 delves into the company's visionary outlook for the future. This chapter explores how Oracle anticipates and embraces emerging technologies and industry trends, positioning itself as a trailblazer in the ever-evolving landscape of digital innovation.

6.1 The Era of Artificial Intelligence and Machine Learning:

The chapter begins by examining Oracle's vision for artificial intelligence (AI) and machine learning (ML). It explores how Oracle incorporates these technologies into its products and services, enabling businesses to harness the power of data-driven insights, automation, and intelligent decision-making.

6.2 Blockchain Technology and Decentralization:

A focal point of Oracle's forward-looking approach is the exploration of blockchain technology and decentralized solutions. This section delves into how Oracle integrates blockchain into its offerings, providing transparency, security, and efficiency in areas such as supply chain management, finance, and beyond.

6.3 Internet of Things (IoT) and Connected Ecosystems:

The narrative then shifts to Oracle's stance on the Internet of Things (IoT) and the vision of a connected ecosystem. This section explores how Oracle enables businesses to leverage IoT data for enhanced visibility, predictive analytics, and improved operational efficiency across various industries.

6.4 Quantum Computing and High-Performance Computing:

As quantum computing emerges as a transformative force, the chapter delves into Oracle's exploration of this cutting-edge technology. It explores Oracle's initiatives in quantum computing and high-performance computing, highlighting their potential to revolutionize complex problem-solving and computational capabilities.

6.5 Cloud-Native Development and Microservices Architecture:

Oracle's commitment to cloud-native development and microservices architecture is explored in this section. It discusses how Oracle facilitates the development of scalable and flexible applications, empowering businesses to adapt to rapidly changing demands and capitalize on cloud-native advantages.

6.6 Edge Computing and Hybrid Cloud:

The chapter unfolds Oracle's perspective on edge computing and the hybrid cloud model. It explores how Oracle supports businesses in distributing computing resources closer to the edge, facilitating real-time processing and analytics while maintaining the flexibility of hybrid cloud environments.

6.7 Industry-Specific Solutions for Digital Transformation:

A critical aspect of Oracle's vision for the future lies in tailoring solutions to industry-specific challenges. This section explores how Oracle continues to innovate in verticals such as healthcare, finance, and manufacturing, providing specialized technologies that drive digital transformation within each sector.

6.8 Ethical and Responsible Technology:

As technology's impact on society grows, the chapter concludes by examining Oracle's commitment to ethical and responsible technology. It explores Oracle's initiatives to address concerns related to data privacy, security, and the responsible use of emerging technologies.

Conclusion:

Chapter 6 provides an insightful exploration of Oracle's vision for the future, encompassing emerging technologies and industry trends. From AI and blockchain to quantum computing and ethical considerations, Oracle's proactive stance positions the company as a thought leader in guiding businesses through the complexities of the digital era. This chapter sets the stage for understanding Oracle's ongoing contributions to shaping the future of enterprise technology.

7

Oracle's Global Impact: Social Responsibility, Diversity, and Corporate Citizenship

Introduction:

As Oracle Corporation continues to shape the technological landscape, Chapter 7 explores the company's global impact beyond the realms of technology. It delves into Oracle's commitment to social responsibility, diversity and inclusion, and corporate citizenship, highlighting how the company endeavors to make a positive difference in the communities it serves.

7.1 Corporate Social Responsibility (CSR) Initiatives:

The chapter begins by examining Oracle's Corporate Social Responsibility (CSR) initiatives. It explores how Oracle channels its resources and expertise to address social challenges, emphasizing areas such as education, environmental sustainability, and community development. The narrative highlights Oracle's commitment to being a responsible corporate citizen on a global scale.

7.2 Education and Skill Development:

A significant aspect of Oracle's social responsibility is its focus on education and skill development. This section explores Oracle's initiatives to bridge the digital skills gap, empower individuals with the knowledge needed for the future workforce, and support educational programs globally.

7.3 Environmental Sustainability:

The chapter delves into Oracle's commitment to environmental sustainability. It explores the company's initiatives to reduce its environmental footprint, increase energy efficiency, and promote sustainable practices in data centers and operations. The narrative underscores Oracle's dedication to minimizing its impact on the planet.

7.4 Diversity and Inclusion:

The narrative then shifts to Oracle's stance on diversity and inclusion. This section explores Oracle's efforts to create a workplace that values diversity in all its forms, fostering an inclusive culture where employees feel empowered and supported. It examines Oracle's initiatives to promote gender equality, diversity in leadership, and an inclusive work environment.

7.5 Philanthropy and Community Engagement:

Philanthropy is a cornerstone of Oracle's commitment to corporate citizenship. This part of the chapter examines Oracle's philanthropic efforts, including charitable donations, volunteer programs, and community engagement initiatives. The narrative underscores how Oracle leverages its resources to make a positive impact on communities worldwide.

7.6 Technology for Social Good:

The chapter unfolds Oracle's initiatives in using technology for social good. It explores how Oracle collaborates with non-profit organizations, governments, and other partners to apply technology solutions to address social challenges, improve public services, and drive positive change.

7.7 Crisis Response and Humanitarian Aid:

As crises unfold around the world, Oracle has been actively involved in providing humanitarian aid and disaster response. This section explores Oracle's initiatives in supporting communities during times of crisis, leveraging its technology, resources, and expertise to make a meaningful difference.

7.8 Measuring Impact and Continuous Improvement:

The chapter concludes by examining how Oracle measures the impact of its social responsibility initiatives and emphasizes the company's commitment to continuous improvement. It discusses Oracle's approach to transparency, accountability, and adapting its strategies to maximize positive outcomes.

Conclusion:

Chapter 7 provides a comprehensive exploration of Oracle's global impact in terms of social responsibility, diversity, and corporate citizenship. As Oracle continues to evolve, its commitment to making a positive contribution to society remains integral to the company's identity. This chapter sets the stage for understanding the broader implications of Oracle's influence beyond the realm of technology.

8

Navigating Challenges and Future Horizons: Oracle in a Dynamic Landscape

Introduction:

As Oracle Corporation navigates through a dynamic and ever-changing technological landscape, Chapter 8 examines the challenges the company has faced and anticipates future horizons. From evolving market trends to technological disruptions, this chapter explores how Oracle continues to adapt, innovate, and shape its strategy for the years ahead.

8.1 Market Dynamics and Competitive Landscape:

The chapter begins by analyzing the market dynamics that Oracle encounters. It explores the competitive landscape, shifting customer expectations, and emerging market trends that influence the company's strategies. The narrative underscores Oracle's agility in adapting to market changes and staying ahead in a competitive environment.

8.2 Technological Disruptions and Innovation:

Technological disruptions are inherent in the fast-paced world of enterprise technology. This section delves into how Oracle responds to disruptive technologies, embraces innovation, and positions itself to lead in areas such as artificial intelligence, machine learning, and emerging computing paradigms.

8.3 Evolving Customer Needs and Industry Shifts:

The narrative then explores how Oracle addresses evolving customer needs and adapts to industry shifts. It examines Oracle's customer-centric approach, the customization of solutions for different industries, and the company's responsiveness to changing business requirements.

8.4 Regulatory and Compliance Challenges:

In the complex landscape of enterprise technology, regulatory and compliance challenges are ever-present. This section explores how Oracle navigates the intricacies of global regulations, data privacy laws, and industry-specific compliance requirements. It underscores Oracle's commitment to maintaining the highest standards of ethical conduct and regulatory compliance.

8.5 Cybersecurity and Data Protection:

With the increasing threat landscape in cybersecurity, this part of the chapter examines how Oracle addresses the challenges of safeguarding data and ensuring the security of its systems. It explores Oracle's cybersecurity initiatives and its role in helping businesses protect their sensitive information from evolving cyber threats.

8.6 Talent Acquisition and Workforce Dynamics:

The success of any technology company relies heavily on its workforce. This section explores how Oracle approaches talent acquisition, workforce development, and the dynamics of a rapidly changing technological landscape.

It delves into Oracle's strategies for attracting and retaining top talent in a competitive industry.

8.7 Global Economic and Geopolitical Factors:

As a global enterprise, Oracle is impacted by economic and geopolitical factors. This part of the chapter analyzes how Oracle navigates the complexities of a global marketplace, considering economic fluctuations, trade policies, and geopolitical shifts that may influence the company's operations and strategy.

8.8 Future Horizons: Oracle's Vision for Tomorrow:

The chapter concludes by offering insights into Oracle's vision for the future. It speculates on the company's potential strategies, innovations, and contributions to the evolving landscape of enterprise technology. By examining Oracle's response to challenges and its forward-looking initiatives, the chapter sets the stage for understanding the company's future trajectory.

Conclusion:

Chapter 8 provides a comprehensive analysis of how Oracle navigates challenges and envisions its future in the dynamic landscape of enterprise technology. From market dynamics to regulatory challenges and future horizons, this chapter encapsulates the resilience and adaptability that define Oracle's ongoing journey. It serves as a fitting conclusion to the exploration of Oracle's impact on the world of technology and business.

9

Reflections and Conclusions: Oracle's Enduring Legacy and the Path Forward

Introduction:

As we culminate our exploration of Oracle Corporation, Chapter 9 offers reflections on the company's enduring legacy, the impact it has had on the world of technology, and a contemplation of the path forward. This chapter serves as a synthesis of the preceding chapters, providing a holistic understanding of Oracle's journey, its contributions, and the broader implications for the future.

9.1 Oracle's Enduring Legacy:

The chapter begins by reflecting on Oracle's enduring legacy. From its humble beginnings as a database company to its current position as a multifaceted technology giant, the narrative delves into the key milestones, innovations, and transformative moments that have shaped Oracle's legacy in the realm of enterprise technology.

9.2 Impact on Enterprise Computing:

An essential aspect of the reflection is an examination of Oracle's impact on enterprise computing. The narrative revisits the company's role in popularizing relational databases, pioneering cloud computing, and driving advancements in business applications. It underscores how Oracle's innovations have influenced the very fabric of how businesses operate and leverage technology.

9.3 Contributions to Database Technology:

The chapter reflects on Oracle's profound contributions to database technology. From the development of the first commercial SQL database to the continuous evolution of Oracle Database, the narrative highlights the pivotal role Oracle has played in advancing the field of database management systems and setting industry standards.

9.4 Transformation through Cloud Computing:

A significant focus of reflection is Oracle's transformative journey into cloud computing. The narrative revisits Oracle's vision for the cloud, the development of comprehensive cloud services, and the company's commitment to providing businesses with the tools they need to thrive in a digital era.

9.5 Social Responsibility and Corporate Citizenship:

The chapter explores Oracle's impact beyond technology, examining the company's commitment to social responsibility and corporate citizenship. It reflects on Oracle's initiatives in education, environmental sustainability, diversity and inclusion, and philanthropy, emphasizing the positive contributions the company makes to society.

9.6 Challenges and Adaptability:

Reflections encompass the challenges Oracle has faced and the company's adaptability in overcoming them. From market dynamics to technological disruptions, the narrative underscores Oracle's resilience and ability to navigate complexities, showcasing the company's agility in an ever-changing landscape.

9.7 Looking Ahead: Oracle's Ongoing Role:

The narrative concludes by looking ahead to Oracle's ongoing role in the world of technology. It speculates on the potential directions the company may take, the innovations it might pioneer, and the impact it could continue to have on enterprise computing, global industries, and societal challenges.

9.8 A Thank You to the Oracle Community:

The chapter includes a note of gratitude to the Oracle community - the users, developers, partners, and enthusiasts who have been an integral part of Oracle's journey. It acknowledges the collaborative spirit that has fueled Oracle's success and expresses appreciation for the diverse contributions that have enriched the Oracle ecosystem.

Conclusion:

Chapter 9 serves as a reflective conclusion to the exploration of Oracle Corporation. It encapsulates the legacy, impact, and ongoing role of Oracle in the world of technology. As we bid farewell to this journey through Oracle's landscape, it leaves the reader with a contemplative perspective on the company's past, present, and the exciting possibilities that lie ahead in the future.

10

Beyond the Horizon: Exploring Emerging Trends and Future Frontiers

Introduction:

In the final chapter, we cast our gaze beyond the present and into the future, exploring emerging trends and future frontiers that are likely to shape Oracle Corporation's trajectory and the broader landscape of enterprise technology. This chapter serves as a forward-looking exploration, delving into the potential transformations, innovations, and challenges that may define the next phase of Oracle's journey.

10.1 The Rise of Quantum Technologies:

As we peer into the future, the chapter initiates with an exploration of the rise of quantum technologies. Quantum computing, in particular, is anticipated to revolutionize computational capabilities. The narrative delves into Oracle's potential role in this emerging field, considering how the company might harness quantum technologies to address complex problems and propel innovation.

10.2 Hyperautomation and Intelligent Processes:

The narrative then shifts to the concept of hyperautomation and intelligent processes. As automation technologies advance, Oracle is likely to play a pivotal role in developing intelligent, self-learning systems that streamline business processes. This section explores how Oracle may contribute to the evolution of hyperautomation, fostering efficiency and agility.

10.3 The Evolution of Augmented Reality (AR) and Virtual Reality (VR):

The chapter explores the evolving landscape of augmented reality (AR) and virtual reality (VR). As these technologies mature, Oracle's applications in industries such as manufacturing, healthcare, and education may expand. The narrative contemplates Oracle's potential contributions to AR and VR, transforming the way businesses engage with digital experiences.

10.4 Edge Computing and Distributed Cloud:

With the increasing importance of real-time data processing, edge computing and distributed cloud architectures come into focus. This section explores how Oracle might navigate the shift towards edge computing, enabling businesses to process data closer to the source and seamlessly integrate distributed cloud environments.

10.5 Ethical AI and Responsible Technology:

As artificial intelligence continues to advance, the chapter delves into the importance of ethical AI and responsible technology. It contemplates Oracle's potential initiatives in ensuring the ethical use of AI, addressing bias, and promoting transparency in algorithmic decision-making.

10.6 Adaptive Cybersecurity and Threat Intelligence:

In the face of evolving cyber threats, the narrative explores the future of adaptive cybersecurity and threat intelligence. Oracle's role in developing advanced cybersecurity solutions that adapt to emerging threats is contemplated, emphasizing the company's commitment to securing digital ecosystems.

10.7 The Continued Integration of Open Source:

Open source technologies are expected to remain integral to the technology landscape. The chapter explores Oracle's ongoing integration of open source solutions, considering how the company may continue to contribute to and leverage open source communities in its products and services.

10.8 Shaping Industry-Specific Solutions:

The chapter concludes by contemplating how Oracle will continue to shape industry-specific solutions. As digital transformation becomes increasingly tailored to specific sectors, Oracle's role in developing customized solutions for industries such as healthcare, finance, and manufacturing is explored.

Conclusion:

Chapter 10 provides a forward-looking exploration of emerging trends and future frontiers that may shape Oracle Corporation's trajectory. As technology continues to evolve, Oracle's commitment to innovation, adaptability, and responsible leadership positions the company to play a transformative role in the unfolding digital landscape. The chapter sets the stage for ongoing curiosity and anticipation of Oracle's contributions to the ever-evolving world of enterprise technology.

11

The Human Element: Oracle's Impact on Workforce Dynamics and the Future of Employment

Introduction:

In this chapter, we turn our attention to the human element and examine Oracle Corporation's impact on workforce dynamics and the evolving landscape of employment. As technology continues to shape the way we work, this chapter explores how Oracle navigates the changing nature of jobs, the role of technology in the workforce, and the company's stance on empowering employees for the future.

11.1 The Evolving Nature of Work:

The chapter begins by delving into the evolving nature of work in the digital age. It explores how technology, automation, and the digital transformation of industries influence the skills and roles demanded in the workforce. Oracle's role in facilitating this evolution and preparing the workforce for the future is examined.

11.2 Oracle's Approach to Talent Acquisition:

Talent acquisition is a critical aspect of workforce dynamics. This section explores Oracle's approach to attracting and retaining top talent. It delves into the company's recruitment strategies, emphasis on diversity and inclusion, and the cultivation of a dynamic and innovative work environment.

11.3 Workforce Development and Continuous Learning:

As the demand for new skills accelerates, the chapter examines Oracle's commitment to workforce development and continuous learning. It explores how Oracle supports its employees in acquiring new skills, adapting to technological advancements, and staying relevant in an ever-changing digital landscape.

11.4 The Role of AI and Automation in Employment:

Automation and artificial intelligence (AI) are reshaping traditional job roles. This section explores Oracle's perspective on the role of AI and automation in employment. It examines how Oracle leverages these technologies to enhance productivity, streamline processes, and create new opportunities within the workforce.

11.5 Remote Work and Digital Collaboration:

The global shift towards remote work has been accelerated by technological advancements. This part of the chapter explores Oracle's approach to remote work and digital collaboration. It delves into the tools and technologies Oracle employs to facilitate seamless communication and collaboration among its distributed workforce.

11.6 Employee Well-being and Work-Life Balance:

Employee well-being and work-life balance have gained prominence in the modern workplace. The chapter explores Oracle's initiatives in promoting a healthy work environment, fostering a positive corporate culture, and supporting employees in achieving a balance between professional and personal life.

11.7 Diversity, Inclusion, and Equity:

Diversity, inclusion, and equity are crucial components of a thriving workplace. This section examines Oracle's commitment to fostering diversity and creating an inclusive environment. It explores the company's initiatives in promoting gender equality, diversity in leadership, and equal opportunities for all employees.

11.8 Adapting to Changing Career Paths:

As career paths become more dynamic, the chapter concludes by exploring how Oracle supports employees in adapting to changing career trajectories. It examines the company's initiatives in mentorship, career development, and creating pathways for employees to explore diverse roles within the organization.

Conclusion:

Chapter 11 provides a comprehensive exploration of Oracle's impact on workforce dynamics and the future of employment. As technology continues to shape the workplace, Oracle's commitment to talent development, diversity, and employee well-being positions the company as a leader in fostering a dynamic and inclusive work environment. This chapter serves as a reflection on Oracle's role in empowering the human element in the digital era.

12

The Global Impact of Oracle: A Retrospective and Prospective View

Introduction:

In this final chapter, we reflect on the global impact of Oracle Corporation, taking a retrospective view of its journey and offering a prospective outlook on the company's future contributions. From its humble beginnings to its current standing as a technology powerhouse, Oracle's influence has extended across industries and geographies. This chapter explores the company's role on the global stage, its contributions to technology, and the potential paths it may tread in the years to come.

12.1 Oracle's Global Reach:

The chapter commences by examining Oracle's global reach. From its origins in Silicon Valley to its presence in diverse markets worldwide, the narrative highlights Oracle's expansive footprint and its impact on businesses, governments, and societies across the globe.

12.2 Industry Transformations:

Oracle has been at the forefront of industry transformations, shaping the way businesses operate and interact. This section reflects on Oracle's role in pivotal moments of change within industries such as finance, healthcare, manufacturing, and more. It explores how Oracle's technologies have become instrumental in driving digital innovation and business resilience.

12.3 The Digital Transformation Journey:

As organizations embark on digital transformation journeys, Oracle has been a key enabler of this paradigm shift. The chapter delves into Oracle's contributions to the digital transformation landscape, examining how the company's technologies have empowered businesses to adapt, innovate, and thrive in an increasingly digital world.

12.4 Oracle's Role in Global Innovation:

Innovation has been a hallmark of Oracle's journey. This section reflects on the company's role in global innovation, from pioneering database technologies to advancing cloud computing, artificial intelligence, and beyond. It explores how Oracle's innovations have not only transformed individual businesses but have also contributed to the broader advancement of technology on a global scale.

12.5 Societal Contributions and Responsibilities:

Beyond technology, Oracle has recognized its societal contributions and responsibilities. This part of the chapter explores Oracle's initiatives in education, environmental sustainability, and community engagement. It reflects on the company's efforts to make a positive impact on a global scale, aligning its strategies with broader societal needs.

12.6 Challenges and Adaptive Strategies:

The chapter reflects on the challenges Oracle has faced throughout its journey and how the company has adapted to navigate these challenges. Whether technological disruptions, market dynamics, or global events, Oracle's resilience and adaptability have played a crucial role in its enduring success.

12.7 Prospective Contributions: Anticipating Oracle's Future Impact:

Looking ahead, the narrative offers a prospective view on Oracle's future impact. It contemplates how Oracle may continue to shape technology landscapes, influence industries, and contribute to global advancements. The chapter speculates on potential areas of growth, innovation, and adaptation in response to emerging trends.

12.8 Oracle's Enduring Values and Culture:

Central to Oracle's global impact is its values and corporate culture. This section reflects on the enduring values that have shaped Oracle's identity and its impact on employees, customers, and partners worldwide. It explores how Oracle's cultural ethos has been a driving force behind its global success.

Conclusion:

Chapter 12 serves as a comprehensive retrospective and prospective view of Oracle Corporation's global impact. From its historical journey to its current standing and potential future contributions, Oracle's role in shaping the global technology landscape is explored. As we conclude this exploration, we are left with a deeper understanding of Oracle's enduring legacy and the dynamic possibilities that lie ahead.

13

Summary

In this comprehensive exploration of Oracle Corporation spanning twelve chapters, we've traced the company's journey from its inception to its current standing as a technology giant with a global impact. The narrative began with Oracle's roots in database technology, showcasing its pivotal role in the development and popularization of relational databases. The story then unfolded through chapters that highlighted Oracle's evolution into cloud computing, enterprise software solutions, and its ecosystem of partnerships and acquisitions.

We delved into Larry Ellison's visionary contributions, explored Oracle's expansive cloud offerings, and scrutinized its impact on enterprise software, workforce dynamics, and social responsibility. Each chapter provided a detailed examination of Oracle's influence in various domains, from database management to cloud services, business applications, and beyond.

The exploration also looked into Oracle's ecosystem, including partnerships, acquisitions, community engagement, and sustainability initiatives. We contemplated Oracle's vision for the future, anticipating its role in emerging technologies and industry trends.

The final chapters reflected on Oracle's impact on workforce dynamics, ethical considerations, and the broader global landscape. The narrative provided insights into Oracle's adaptability, resilience, and commitment to a diverse, inclusive, and socially responsible corporate culture.

As we looked ahead, the exploration considered emerging trends, future frontiers, and the potential paths Oracle might take in shaping the digital era. The concluding chapters offered a retrospective and prospective view, examining Oracle's global reach, industry transformations, societal contributions, and adaptive strategies in the face of challenges.

Throughout this journey, the narrative emphasized Oracle's enduring legacy, innovative spirit, and impact on the world of technology. Whether through pioneering database technologies, transformative cloud services, or societal contributions, Oracle's influence has been profound, leaving an indelible mark on the past, present, and future of enterprise technology.

www.ingramcontent.com/pod-product-compliance
Lightning Source LLC
LaVergne TN
LVHW010440070526
838199LV00066B/6101